Great Danes

By Kristen Rajczak

Gareth Stevens
Publishing

Please visit our website, www.garethstevens.com. For a free color catalog of all our high-quality books, call toll free 1-800-542-2595 or fax 1-877-542-2596.

Library of Congress Cataloging-in-Publication Data

Rajczak, Kristen.
Great danes / Kristen Rajczak.
    p. cm. — (Great big dogs)
Includes index.
ISBN 978-1-4339-5776-5 (pbk.)
ISBN 978-1-4339-5777-2 (6-pack)
ISBN 978-1-4339-5774-1 (library binding)
1. Great Dane—Juvenile literature. I. Title.
SF429.G7R35 2011
636.73—dc22

                                2010046048

First Edition

Published in 2012 by
Gareth Stevens Publishing
111 East 14th Street, Suite 349
New York, NY 10003

Copyright © 2012 Gareth Stevens Publishing

Designer: Andrea Davison-Bartolotta
Editor: Kristen Rajczak

Photo credits: Cover, pp. 1, 13 iStockphoto.com; pp. 5, 20 Shutterstock.com; p. 6 H. Armstrong Roberts/Getty Images; p. 9 George Doyle/Stockbyte/Thinkstock; p. 10 DreamPictures/Getty Images; p. 14 Siri Stafford/Photodisc/Thinkstock; p. 17 Eric Charbonneau/Le Studio/WireImage/Getty Images; p. 18 Hiroko Masuike/Getty Images.

Printed in the United States of America

CPSIA compliance information: Batch #CS11GS: For further information contact Gareth Stevens, New York, New York at 1-800-542-2595.

Contents

An Old Breed 4

History of Hunters 7

Family Companion 8

Gentle Giant 11

Big and Beautiful 12

Dependable Dog 15

Marmaduke. 16

Scooby-Doo. 19

Owning a Great Dane 20

Glossary 22

For More Information 23

Index 24

Words in the glossary appear in **bold** type the first time they are used in the text.

An Old Breed

Great Danes look much like dogs that lived thousands of years ago. More than 5,000 years ago, Egyptians made drawings of dogs that were large like Great Danes. A **breed** like the Great Dane was also written about in ancient Chinese books. However, the lovable dog we know as the Great Dane looks and acts differently from these ancient dogs. The modern Great Dane took shape in Germany during the 1600s.

Dog Tales

People from the country of Denmark are called Danes, but the Great Dane isn't from Denmark.

◁ The Great Dane breed has a long history.

Dog Tales

Boar hunters first **cropped** Great Danes' ears to stop them from being hurt by the animals they hunted.

Though Great Danes were often hunters in the past, today they are more common as pets.

History of Hunters

Early Great Danes were smaller and more **muscular** than the long-legged Great Danes of today. They were used during the 1500s in England and Germany to hunt wild boars, which are mean, pig-like animals. These "boar hounds" were bred from English **mastiffs** and Irish wolfhounds.

During the 1600s, German nobles started using the biggest of the boar hounds to keep their homes safe. The dogs started to change from a breed of hunters to wonderful companions and pets.

7

Family Companion

The Great Danes of German nobles looked like a separate breed from the boar-hunting mastiffs. These Great Danes were tall and lean. They also had the sweet nature of today's Great Danes.

A Great Dane loves nothing more than being with its family. It will guard them like a mother dog guards her puppies. Great Danes are very playful and friendly. They like children—even though Great Danes are bigger than most children!

Dog Tales

The Great Dane was named the national dog of Germany in 1876. They called it *Deutsche dogge,* which means "German mastiff."

Great Danes like to be close to their families.

Dog Tales

As of October 2010, the tallest dog alive was a Great Dane named Giant George. Giant George is 43 inches (1.1 m) tall at the shoulder, according to Guinness World Records.

When standing on its back legs, a Great Dane can be taller than a person!

Gentle Giant

The most noticeable thing about a Great Dane is its size. A fully grown Great Dane is often 28 to 34 inches (71 to 86 cm) tall at the shoulder and weighs 100 to 200 pounds (45 to 90 kg). However, it's hard to guess how big a Great Dane will be when it's fully grown. A puppy can weigh as much as 65 pounds (30 kg) at 4 months old. By the time a Great Dane is a year old, it might already weigh 140 pounds (64 kg)!

Big and Beautiful

Great Danes are good-looking dogs. They have smooth, shiny coats. Their fur is short and can be many colors. Some Great Danes are black or gold. Others are **brindle**, **harlequin,** or **fawn**.

Great Danes have long front legs and a powerful chest. They're born with large ears that fall forward. Some owners crop their dog's ears so they stand up straight on top of the dog's head.

These Great Danes have had their ears cropped.

13

Dog Tales

Great Danes are calm dogs, but sometimes puppies run around in circles. This is called getting the "zoomies."

According to the American Kennel Club, Great Danes were the 21st most popular dog in 2009.

14

Dependable Dog

Great Danes have quiet natures. This makes them good **service dogs**. Some Great Danes are trained to visit with sick or lonely people to cheer them up. Others help people who don't move well. They're strong and can learn how to push wheelchairs and open doors.

Great Danes are perfect watchdogs for families. If something isn't right, a Great Dane will give a powerful bark. Its size can be scary to burglars, too!

Marmaduke

Marmaduke is a Great Dane who always gets into trouble. Brad Anderson has been drawing him in the **comic strip** *Marmaduke* since 1954. The comic is printed in newspapers all over the world. More than 20,000 *Marmaduke* comic strips have been printed! There are more than 20 books of *Marmaduke* comics, too. Actor Owen Wilson was the voice of the famous Great Dane in the movie *Marmaduke* in 2010.

This Great Dane played comic-strip dog Marmaduke in a movie.

17

Dog Tales

Radio star Casey Kasem has been doing the voice of Scooby's best friend, Shaggy, since the very beginning of the TV show.

Scooby-Doo is so popular he has had his own balloon in the Macy's Thanksgiving Day Parade!

18

Scooby-Doo

This funny cartoon dog is a Great Dane! Scooby-Doo and his friends have been uncovering mysteries on TV for more than 40 years. The TV show *Scooby-Doo, Where Are You!* started in 1969. There have been many movies starring Scooby since then. Two of these include *Scooby-Doo*, which came out in 2002, and the 2004 movie *Scooby-Doo 2: Monsters Unleashed*. Scooby-Doo is known for his love of food. Like Scooby, all Great Danes like to eat a lot!

Owning a Great Dane

Great Dane puppies need training because of their size. They need to be walked every day, too. These dogs will sleep on the couch all day if their owners let them! However, Great Danes should not be exercised too much. Their large bodies cause them to get tired more quickly than small dogs.

Some owners take their Great Danes to dog shows. They are judged on looks and how well they do tasks. Everywhere they go, these dogs are noticed!

Learning About Great Danes

height	28 to 34 inches (71 to 86 cm)
weight	100 to 200 pounds (45 to 90 kg)
coloring	black, gold, brindle, harlequin, fawn
life span	7 to 10 years

Glossary

breed: a group of animals that share features different from other groups of the kind

brindle: uneven dark bands on lighter-colored fur

comic strip: one part of a cartoon's story printed in a book, newspaper, magazine, or online

crop: to cut off part of the outside of the ear so that it stands up

fawn: a light grayish brown

harlequin: fur of one color with uneven spots of another color

mastiff: a large, powerful dog that has a smooth coat

muscular: having large muscles, the parts of the body that allow movement

service dog: a dog that is trained to help people who do not hear, see, or move well

For More Information

Books

Fiedler, Julie. *Great Danes.* New York, NY: PowerKids Press, 2006.

Hart, Joyce. *Big Dogs.* New York, NY: Marshall Cavendish Benchmark, 2008.

Websites

Great Dane Club of America
www.gdca.org/before.htm
Learn more about owning a Great Dane.

Woof! It's a Dog's Life
www.pbs.org/wgbh/woof/
Play games and read stories about being a dog owner.

Index

American Kennel Club 14

boar hounds 7, 8

boars 6, 7

breed 4, 5, 7, 8

China 4

coat 12

Denmark 5

Deutsche dogge 9

dog shows 20

ears 6, 12, 13

Egypt 4

England 7

exercise 20

family 8, 9, 15

fur 12

Germany 4, 7, 8, 9

Giant George 10

Guinness World Records 10

hunters 6, 7

Irish wolfhounds 7

Marmaduke 16, 17

Marmaduke 16

mastiffs 7, 8, 9

pets 6, 7

Scooby-Doo 18, 19

Scooby-Doo 19

Scooby-Doo 2: Monsters Unleashed 19

Scooby-Doo, Where Are You! 19

service dogs 15

training 15, 20

watchdogs 15

"zoomies" 14